WALKING OUT OF THE SHADOW OF PAIN

Volume #1   A Guide for Addressing Mental Health, Grief, Loss, Anxiety, Depression, and Trauma in The Church

Includes portions of my journey with grief, loss, and depression. You can survive pain, despair, and loss, and move forward into experiencing renewed hope, peace, and victory.

DR. ANTHONY WALTON

Walking out of the Shadow of Pain
Copyright © Anthony Walton 2023

All rights reserved. No part of this publication may be reproduced, stored, or introduced into a retrieval system, communicated or transmitted, in any form or by any means (electronic, mechanical, photocopying recording, or otherwise), without the prior written permission of the copyright owner and the publisher of this book.

All scripture references, unless otherwise indicated, are taken from the King James Version of the Holy Bible.

"*Despite his deep desire to overcome mental illness and lead others out of their own pain, pastor Andrew Stoecklein died by suicide at the age of thirty.*" (Stoecklein, 2020)

    Stoecklein, K. (2020). Fear gone wild: A Story of mental illness, suicide, and hope through loss. Nelson Books.

Table of Contents

THE PURPOSE 7
Introduction 9
Chapter 1 You and Your Health 11
Chapter 2 Five Myths About Mental Illness 15
Chapter 3 Mental Health 16
Chapter 4 When Mental Health Goes Undiagnosed in the Church 17
Chapter 5 Showing Affection In The Church 20
Chapter 6 Mental Health and Medication 22
Chapter 7 Mental Health and Children 23
Chapter 8 Grief – What is It? 26
Chapter 9 Why am I feeling like this? 27
Chapter 10 Warning Signs and Types of Depression 33
Chapter 11 The Impact of Death on the Family System - Financial Planning 38
Chapter 12 Sharing My Loss 40
Chapter 13 "The Empty Quiver" Excerpt 42
Chapter 14 The Anger and the Loss of a Desire to Pray 43
Chapter 15 Types of Grief 46
Chapter 16 Stages of Grief 47
Chapter 17 Reacting to the Grief or Loss 51
Chapter 18 The Accepting of God's Will 53
Chapter 19 Moving Forward 54

Chapter 20 Grief and Loss in the Church 56

Chapter 21 Questions I Am Often Asked About Grief Loss and Depression 57

Chapter 22 You Do Not Have To Be Superman - Allowing You To Be You 66

Chapter 23 Addressing Trauma and PTSD 69

Chapter 24 Tips for working through your Grief, Anxiety, Depression, and Trauma 72

Chapter 25 Suicide Ideations 74

Chapter 26 My Crisis Plan 76

Chapter 27 Resources for Getting Mental Health Help 78

References 81

THE PURPOSE

The purpose of this book is to encourage and educate those who may be experiencing personal mental health issues, or desire to assist someone else who has experienced a personal loss, to be able to move forward. I have included several references from my book "The Empty Quiver". Many of those who read the book shared with me what they enjoyed most from the book and others have expressed a desire for more informational resources that would be of help to them in addressing their loss.

As in my previous book, I talked about challenges, heartaches, and pains anyone who has or may currently be experiencing grief due to any kind of a loss either great or small, can find themselves struggling to overcome.

I will share with the readers the journey my wife and I experienced, which stretched us to the limit and beyond what we thought we could ever handle individually or as a couple.

This book has been designed to address mental health issues as well as explain what grief and loss or and allow the reader to explore, identify, and understand what stage of grief and loss he or she may currently be experiencing.

Introduction

For far too long we have long overlooked the need to address the subject of mental health in the church. For many Christians, the thought of a Christian experiencing any kind of mental crisis is considered a subject they refuse to face.

As a therapist, I have seen too many well-intended Christians neglect the mental health of their loved ones as well as in many cases their mental health.

We often try to rationalize or spiritualize any kind of unnormal behavior. We always say it's just Satan. While Satan is manifesting his spirit in the area of mental health, there is also a natural manifestation that must be addressed as well.

We can no longer expect to have a healthy church until we fully identify, address and recognize the mental health challenges within the church.

We must recognize there are countless members in our churches who are suffering in silence either afraid to or unaware of how to address their mental health concerns.

It is my desire is that this book will become a starting point for further discussions in this area.

Chapter 1
You and Your Health

Just how seriously do you take your health? For many of us, we have come to learn the importance of focusing on our physical health. We exercise, we go to the gym regularly. It appears the message has gotten out about the importance of bodily health and exercise. But this was not always the case for many Christians.

Previously for many Christians, we did not take bodily exercise seriously at all. Christians were notorious for poor health, poor eating habits, and all around not maintaining a balance when it came to addressing and maintaining our good health.

One of the reasons many Christians neglected their health was that going to the doctor was frowned upon. One of the scriptures in the bible used to support this line of thought is *"For bodily exercise profiteth little: but godliness is profitable unto all things, having promise of the life that now is, and of that which is to come."* ***1 Timothy 4:8 KJV.*** Some Christians used this reference to indicate that exercise and focusing on our health were not of much real value. It was looked down upon because it was felt that if a person went to the doctor, it showed a lack of faith in the ability of God to heal them. There are many today who still hold to this belief and will refuse to go to the doctor for any reason. However, many have come to realize that going to the doctor for a check-up does not diminish their faith in God. Going to the doctor for checkups has allowed for the prevention of many diseases and sicknesses that would have otherwise gone unnoticed leading to further illnesses or even death.

Many churches today promote self-awareness and self-care. Many churches have gymnasiums where their members can get together and fellowship and work out with other believers to maintain better health.

While it appears that going to the doctor for our physical health has finally become acceptable in Christian circles it seems that the idea of our emotional health has not. For some Christians, it would be unheard of for them to see a mental health professional.

I can remember while I was in grad school working on my degree in counseling, I had a conversation with someone who adamantly opposed any Christians going to a doctor for their mental health. Further, they could not understand why I as a Christian would even want to go into the field of mental health. I explained to them some many Christians are experiencing various mental health stresses and while you can pray for some of them, and they can immediately experience a breakthrough. For others, their needs are much more serious as they often have many layers affecting their emotional condition that must be uncovered before they can receive a breakthrough. Now that is not to say they cannot be delivered through prayer, but some are at a point where they either need therapeutic therapy or may even need medication to help them balance their emotional state.

Chapter 2
Five Myths About Mental Illness

Mental Illness Doesn't Exist

Depression Is a Sign of Weak Faith

All Mental Health Issues Can Be Prayed Away

My Community Won't Understand My Mental Health Needs

People with Mental Illnesses are Unstable and Unfit for Church Leadership

Chapter 3
Mental Health

"Mental illnesses are common in the United States. It is estimated that more than one in five U.S. adults live with a mental illness (57.8 million in 2021). Mental illnesses include many different conditions that vary in degree of severity, ranging from mild to moderate to severe. Two broad categories can be used to describe these conditions: Any Mental Illness (AMI) and Serious Mental Illness (SMI). AMI encompasses all recognized mental illnesses. SMI is a smaller and more severe subset of AMI." National Institute on Mental Health

Chapter 4
When Mental Health Goes Undiagnosed in the Church

"But in a great house, there are not only vessels of gold and of silver, but also of wood and of earth; and some to honour, and some to dishonour. 21 If a man therefore purge himself from these, he shall be a vessel unto honour, sanctified, and meet for the master's use, and prepared unto every good work." 2 Timothy 2:20-21 KJV

We must never forget the mission of the church. The church is a place for forgiveness, healing, restoration, and deliverance. When we come together in the house of God we must not forget that we are all full of imperfections. If we are not careful, we will come to over-expect from others and eventually come up disappointed.

We must realize there are a lot of hurting and wounded people in the church. Some have been verbally, mentally, emotionally, and physically abused. They come into the church from all walks of life, with baggage wanting to be healed spiritually and emotionally. If we only focus on a single area of their deliverance, we can miss and not address the actual need that they may have.

As the scripture tells us, in that great house there are all types of vessels (referring to people) some of honor and some of less honor. It is up to that individual as he or she seeks God to receive the type of healing they need. We must be keenly aware that many of those coming into the church not only need our prayers but our wisdom to direct them to the proper sources for them to receive what they need.

Too many people in the church with emotional and mental illnesses or trauma or simply dismissed as saying "They are just filled with the devil".

I remember a member of a church who would often go out of their way to speak to me. But the next time I would see them it was as if they did just the opposite. It was as if they went out of their way not to speak with me. I was perplexed by their actions and wonder if I had done something to offend them. I was later talking with that person, and they shared we me how they often suffered from bipolar.

We should never be quick to judge the actions of others until we do further investigation.

There are many people in our churches that are masking their emotional hurt. Many are suffering in silence for fear of being misunderstood or ostracized by the church. The church must be a haven for those suffering from mental illness to be able to safely and without shame address the many challenges they are facing daily.

Chapter 5
Showing Affection In The Church

The church is often known as a place where people freely show affection towards one another. For many of us, that is not a problem. I had a client who shared with me how she had been sexually assaulted by someone in the church and many times whenever a male would touch her even a simple touch on the shoulder, it would be a trigger of her past traumas. The sad thing about it is for those who were unaware of her situation and if she had gone undiagnosed then she would have easily been perceived as standoffish or unfriendly. We should never be quick to judge others in the church before we know their story.

Different Personality Types

A person's personality type can be a very important indicator of how he or she perceives those around them. Some people are more sensitive than others and their sensitivity causes them to receive things differently than others. Some suffer from paranoia which further affects their perception. Some introverts have chosen to close themselves off from others as a defense mechanism to prevent them from being hurt. (many of these have suffered past trauma which causes them to shut themselves off from others.)

Many extroverts have a hard time trusting someone who is introverted thinking they may have something to hide, while introverts are often leery of extroverts because many of them to the introvert appear to be overly aggressive.

Our personality type and past life experience impact in a major way how we are perceived by others as well as how we perceive others.

Chapter 6
Mental Health and Medication

One of the first things a doctor or therapist will do with a new client is to give them an assessment. Many medications we take can have side effects that can affect our mood. If a person is taking the wrong medication or even the wrong dosage it can affect their mental capacity and if gone unchecked could lead to a misdiagnosis of that individual's mental state.

You should always check your medications before you overreact to your emotions. Many medications themselves can be mood-altering and cause a person to experience depression.

Chapter 7
Mental Health and Children

As I counsel many kids and young people, unfortunately, I find that many of them are suffering from similar mental diagnoses as their adult parents.

Many of the kids I counsel, some as young as four years old, are experiencing signs of anxiety, depression, attention deficit, as well as many other mental illnesses.

This becomes a major problem when the family has a history of mental illness. Often there are some co-morbidities associated with the home.

During the pandemic, I had to counsel both the adult and the child in many situations where the parents became exasperated with trying to care for a child, which in many cases was suffering from ADHD or Autism, with both requiring a lot of attention on the part of the parents or caregiver.

When it comes to Attention Deficit Hyper Disorder (ADHD) many of the children were described various types of medicines. For some, the medicine worked and for others, it changed the behavior of the child but not always for the best.

It is important to realize that children can often be helped significantly with medication and therapy. I had many successes working with young children suffering from either ADHD or autism.

In many churches, I have found there are a lot of grandparents who for one reason or another end up assuming a lot of the responsibility for the care of their grandchild. This adds further mental strain on the grandparent as a caregiver, becoming overloaded with this responsibility and now finding themselves suffering from mental stress and anxiety. Often these grandparents are sitting in our churches not sharing the challenges they are experiencing but themselves needing therapeutic intervention.

ADHD is one of the most common neurodevelopmental disorders of childhood. It is usually first diagnosed in childhood and often lasts into adulthood. Children with ADHD may have trouble paying attention, control impulsive behaviors (may act without thinking about what the result will be) or be overly active.

Autism spectrum disorder (ASD) is a developmental disability caused by differences in the brain. Some people with ASD have a known difference, such as a genetic condition. Other causes are not yet known.

Chapter 8

Grief – What is It?

When people talk about the word "Grief,". They usually are referring to the pain and hurt they may experience after the loss of a family member or loved one.

Grief normally implies how we are affected by the various ranges of emotions we feel. As we experience these emotions in this process, we are considered to be going through bereavement.

"Three out of four women outlive their spouse, with the average age of becoming a widow being 56 years. More than half of women in the United States are widowed by the time they reach age 65. Every year in the United States, 4% of children under the age of 15 experience the loss of a parent through death."

https://www.medicinenet.com/loss_grief_and_bereavement/article.htm)

Chapter 9
Why am I feeling like this?

Experiencing certain kinds of grief is a part of life for most of us. We experience it at different levels at different times. We can grieve over the death of a friend, or a loved one, or even about things such as a pet, car, house, pictures, a job, and the list goes on. Anything that we hold near and dear to our hearts if taken away from us can be considered a major loss and a cause to grieve.

I can remember when I was facilitating a group session, one of the members in the group shared with me how he was grieving because of knowing that he would soon have to put his dog to sleep. I quickly recognized he was experiencing the same sense of loss as someone who may have lost a family member.

We should never normalize grief., we should be aware, how we process our losses may be completely different than someone else.

I recently experienced how a family member got upset with another member in his family over the loss of a parent because. One family member was struggling to be able to process the loss as it appeared to him that the other member had been able to quickly move on. While the other found himself continuing to experience constant pain and hurt daily. Whenever this happens there can be negative feelings and resentment on the part of one individual toward the other. One is upset due to feelings of hurt, isolation, pain, emptiness, despair, abandonment, and a whole host of other negative feelings, while the other may feel disapproval from the other for them being able to make the adjustment and move on. *(I would note that I share that the other appeared to move on. I used the word <u>appeared</u> because you can never simply look at how a person reacts and know the full truth or degree of the pain they are experiencing.)*

While experiencing the pain and hurt and emotions associated with grief, we will most often ask ourselves the question "Why am I feeling this way?" We search for answers to validate the emotions we are feeling at that time. For many, the answers never seem to come. When we do not get the answers we want, our grief can turn into depression, anger, and or a sense of despair. We search and search for answers to explain the reason why we are feeling the way we do. However, what we are experiencing is a feeling that can often be unable to explain or even verbalize.

For many, the pain they experience is as if someone has driven a dagger straight through their heart. For others, it is as if a heavy weight has been dropped down on them. For some, their loss simply leaves them with a sense of feeling completely numb not knowing exactly how they feel.

The reason we feel the way we do can sometimes be found in our attachment style. Well, what does that have to do with anything?

I write in my book *"The Window to Understanding And Building Healthy Relationships," Attachment Styles* refer to a child's relationship with and need for his/her caregiver(s), which sets the tone for all future relationship patterns and interactions. In other words, how close you were to your parents growing up or how distant you were can play an important part in how affectionate a person will be in later life, or how distant and sometimes how clingy they may be in other relationships.

When we have a healthy attachment, we can find ourselves becoming more attached to others, especially our parents. When this attachment is broken there is often a sense of loss, and the separation can become so damaging it is can be as if the person experiencing the loss may feel as if the person or thing they lost were a part of them physically. It is as if you were hanging on to a rope with someone holding the other end and suddenly the person lets go of the rope. Now you are feeling hurt, vulnerable, and sometimes even afraid of what the future may hold. You imagined that this person or thing would be with you forever or at the least for a longer extent of time, only to be awakened to a new reality without that person or the thing you held near and dear to your heart.

Another reason we asked the question "Why am I feeling like this? is because some individuals have unresolved issues with the person they have lost. They do not feel a sense of closure that he or she would have liked to have had with the person they lost. They never got to have that last conversation, the one they would now be willing to exchange almost anything for. Often the thought is If I only had one more chance to spend some time, even if just for a little while, with the person I cared so much for I would do anything. *We should value every moment we have with our loved ones as if it could be the last time, we may see him or them.*

We are all human beings and however you feel, you must realize your feelings and emotions are a part of who you are. Whenever you compare your actions to the actions of someone else who may have experienced a similar loss as yours, you must realize you are two different individuals with different experiences and different emotions. You should not allow yourself or anyone else to compare how you respond to your loss, to how they may feel they would have responded to your loss.

You feel the way you are because you are unique, and we can never normalize any kind of loss, and at the time we can find it difficult to control our emotions when we are hurting. Regardless of how long it takes, we must allow ourselves enough time to process the loss. For some it may be weeks, for others, it may be months, and for some, it may even be years. You must realize that everyone processes their loss differently and over different periods.

Chapter 10
Warning Signs and Types of Depression

<u>Depression</u> is not just feeling blue from time to time. Instead, the warning signs of <u>depression</u> are characterized by overwhelming daily feelings of sadness, hopelessness, worthlessness, and emptiness. A person who experiences depression often cannot see a future for themselves — they may feel like the world is closing in around them.

Depression Warning Signs
Not everyone who is depressed experiences all of the following warning signs, some people will experience a few signs, while others may experience more. The severity of symptoms varies with individuals and also varies over time. These signs are usually pretty clear to those around the person suffering — the person doesn't seem at all like their normal self. The changes in the person's mood are (usually) evident to friends and family.

      Symptoms of Depression
- Persistent sad, anxious, or empty mood
- Feelings of hopelessness, pessimism
- Feelings of guilt, worthlessness, helplessness

- Loss of interest or pleasure in hobbies and activities that were once enjoyed, including sex
- Decreased energy, fatigue, being "slowed"
- Difficulty concentrating, remembering, or making decisions.
- Insomnia, early-morning awakening, or oversleeping
- Appetite and/or weight loss or overeating and weight gain.
- Thoughts of death or suicide; suicide attempts
- Restlessness, irritability
- Persistent physical symptoms that do not respond to treatment, such as headaches, digestive disorders, and chronic pain.

For depression to be diagnosed, the person must experience these symptoms every day, for at least 2 weeks.

Types of Depression

Major Depressive Disorder
Dysthymia
Adjustment Disorder with Depressed Mood.
Seasonal depression is called **seasonal affective disorder** (SAD).
Bipolar disorder.
Grief, mourning, and deprivation.

Bereavement is the state of experiencing grief, mourning, and deprivation as the result of a loss, usually death.

ANXIETY WHEEL

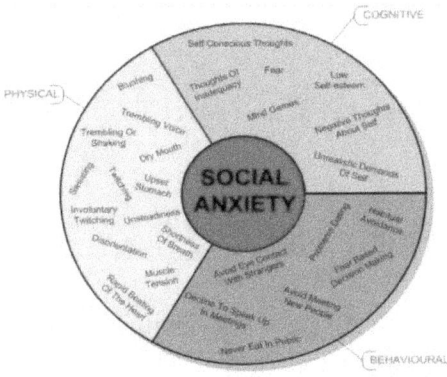

The wheel represents the actions and emotions of those experiencing Social Anxiety

Thoughts

Feelings

BEHAVIOR

This is a common method to identify thoughts, feelings, and corresponding behaviors.

National Center for Health Statistics

Depression

MORBIDITY

- Percent of adults aged 18 and over with regular feelings of depression: 4.7%

PHYSICIANS OFFICE VISITS

- Number of physician office visits with depressive disorders as the primary diagnosis: 15.0 million

- Percent of physician office visits with depression indicated on the medical record: 11.0%

EMERGENCY DEPARTMENT VISITS

- Percent of emergency department visits with depression indicated on the medical record: 12.7%

MORTALITY

- number of suicide deaths: 48,183
- Suicide deaths per 100,000 population: 14.5

If you or someone you know is grieving, it may help to express your thoughts and feelings openly or through writing, and journaling.

<u>Speak openly</u> with other family members who suffered the same loss - Accept and allow a range of emotions - seek professional help for overwhelming feelings or trouble returning to daily activities over time.

Chapter 11
The Impact of Death on the Family System - Financial Planning

"The impact of death on the family system creates a structural void that requires homeostatic adjustments. A family member may be stuck in one of the phases of grieving." (Journal of Family Therapy (1983) 5: 279 294)

There are many factors to consider when talking about the impact death has on the family system such as economic impact, emotional impact, childcare, financial literacy and so much more, All these factors way on those experiencing the loss as they grieve over their love ones and attempt to move forward.

Anyone of these factors can lead to mental illnesses such as stress, anxiety, depression as well a host of other illnesses.

Many people get stuck after the passing of a loved one, fearful of moving forward especially when they may not have been involved in many of the business aspects of the relationship. For example, some spouses are content to let the other person handle the checkbook and now that person is gone from their life, they are clueless as to what to do next. At this point, they must experience a new norm to make the proper adjustments.

Financial planning is so important in considering your family after your death. Make sure others know your final wishes and have them written in writing and authorized. This will cut down a lot of friction between family members after your death.

Chapter 12
Sharing My Loss

My wife and I were a young newlywed couple when we found out she was pregnant. We were extremely excited and anticipated becoming parents. Our excitement was short-lived when my wife delivered our son prematurely. This was devastating to both my wife and me. Something we could have never imagined in our worst nightmare.

When our son was born the doctor gave him little chance of surviving the delivery but to our amazement, he survived. We named our son Anthony Christopher Walton. I do not have a middle name so Christopher would distinguish him from myself. We were once again excited with the hope that he would overcome the challenges of being premature and have the prospect of a normal life. The more time we spent with him the closer attached we both became to him.

About three months after the birth of our son he took a turn for the worst and died. Our world was literally turned upside down.

Chapter 13
"The Empty Quiver" Excerpt

(Excerpt from the book "THE EMPTY QUIVER")

WHEN THE QUESTION TO GOD IS, "WHY?"

I always felt I was strong in my faith up until this time. I would share my faith with anyone willing to listen. I spoke with many individuals who questioned their faith in God, and I would tell them that what they were going through was just a test of their faith. I would tell them, "You can make it! Just keep the faith!"

Somehow, when Shirley and I were going through our test, I found myself questioning my faith in God and everything I knew regarding God, up to this point. I kept asking myself, "If you love me, God, and I have done all I can do to live a Godly life, then why God, did you let this happen to us?"

I was angry, mad, hurt, disappointed, and frustrated. I knew Satan was trying his best to get me to the place where I would begin to consider giving up on my faith in the church as well as in God.

I began to ask God, "Why me, why my family, why my little son?" I even asked God why he couldn't have taken me and let my son live. So many things ran through my mind as I began to relive over, and, over, and over again the events of the previous seven to eight months.

Chapter 14

The Anger and the Loss of a Desire to Pray

(More excerpts from the book "THE EMPTY QUIVER")

THE ANGER AND THE LOSS OF DESIRE TO PRAY

I was angry for many reasons. Primarily because of the loss of my son, but secondly because of the responses from many of the Christians who showed very little, if any, concern for our situation. I thought the church would embrace us, only to find out that many of those whom I thought were our friends did not even reach out to us to show any sympathy or concern.

I found myself dealing with all kinds of emotions. I did not know exactly how to feel. How should I have felt? Should I just go on with my life as before or should I be angry with God? I did not know what to do with myself.

I tried to pray, and I could not find the right words to say. I rehearsed in my mind, the scripture; "***Give thanks in every***

"***And he spake a parable unto them to this end, that men ought always to pray, and not to faint;***"

(*Luke 18:1, King James Version*)

There were those individuals who just blatantly asked, "What do you think is wrong? What have you or Shirley done to bring this upon you?" I now know in the midst of all I was going through, God had his hand on me, or I would have expressed to these individuals just how I felt. At this space in time, I am not sure just how spiritual my response would have been. Thank God for having his hand over my life even when I did not realize it.

I was not sure what to do, but I knew I could not give up on God. I had to trust in Him, I had to hold on to see what His ultimate divine plan was for Shirley and me.

"O lord, thou hast searched me, and known me. Thou knowest my downsitting and mine uprising, thou understandest my thought afar off. Thou compassest my path and my lying down, and art acquainted with all my ways. For there is not a word in my tongue, but, lo, O LORD, thou knowest it altogether. Thou hast beset me behind and before, and laid thine hand upon me. Such knowledge is too wonderful for me; it is high, I cannot attain unto it. Whither shall I go from thy spirit? or whither shall I flee from thy presence? If I ascend up into heaven, thou art there: if I make my bed in hell, behold, thou art there. If I take the wings of the morning, and dwell in the uttermost parts of the sea; even there shall thy hand lead me, and thy right hand shall hold me."
(*Psalms 139:1-10, King James Version*)

Grief is a natural human **response** to the **loss** of a loved one. It can show itself in many ways. **Grief** moves in and out of stages from disbelief and denial to anger and guilt, to finding a source of comfort, to eventually adjusting to the loss.

"Depression in men often goes undiagnosed or improperly treated because of unique qualities that make it different from depression in women. depression in men is not strictly the product of major life events; it also regularly appears in response to minor troubling issues that often go entirely overlooked by others or, if recognized at all, are downplayed" (Kantor, M. (2007)

Chapter 15
Types of Grief

EIGHT TYPES OF GRIEF:

1. Anticipatory grief

2. Normal or common grief

3. Complicated grief

4. Delayed grief

5. Inhibited grief

6. Disenfranchised grief

7. Absent grief

8. Seasonal Depression

Chapter 16
Stages of Grief

There are several stages an individual may experience as they go through the grief process. Some say there are five stages whereas others must include up to seven or even eight stages. I will address the most common stages I have encountered when addressing many of my clients who are experiencing grief.

I like the definition of the stages of grief as defined by According to gatewaycounseling.com/7-stages-of-grief-explained:

SEVEN STAGES OF GRIEF:

1. **DISBELIEF & SHOCK**

The initial reaction to loss includes a feeling of shock. Learning someone you love is gone creates numbness and fills a person with doubt. This is a form of emotional protection and can last for weeks. The time experienced often reflects the suddenness of the death, but there is no cookie-cutter recipe for grief. It's not uncommon for someone to go through the shock phase throughout the process of going through the funeral.

2. DENIAL

The next stage of grief reflects the stubbornness of the human spirit. The mind goes into a state of denial to avoid the pain and reality of loss. A person can deny a loved one's passing for weeks no matter the circumstances around the death. People experience other kinds of denial as well. For instance, a grieving person may deny that the loss seriously affects them. Denial is a type of self-preservation much like a shock. A person's experience with the stage helps shelter them from the eventual pain and ensuing stages of grief.

3. GUILT AND PAIN

As a person begins to feel the full realization of someone's death, their numbness leads the way to extreme emotional pain and suffering. Guilt often accompanies this pain. A person may feel survivor's guilt or a constant sense of "what might have been." They may feel remorse over missed opportunities or things they did or didn't do with their loved ones before their passing. It's important to experience the full depth of pain when going through grief. Masking this stage with alcohol or drugs only makes things worse in the long run.

4.   BARGAINING

The negotiation phase occurs when a grieving person needs an emotional release from the shock and pain of loss. This phase involves wrestling with fate or "the powers that be" to try and make sense of loss. Of course, there is nothing one can do to bring someone back from the dead.

5.   ANGER

People going through this phase tend to lash out at the ones around them as an unwarranted reaction to the feelings of helplessness. One may place undue blame on someone else for the death. Grief strains the relationships of the living. To preserve these relationships, it's imperative to find a way to release these extreme emotions healthily. Failing to do so may permanently damage ties you have with friends, family, or coworkers.

6. DEPRESSION

People who never experienced depression before have a hard time with this stage. Depression is all-encompassing and consumes your life. While it may seem extreme and worrying to go through a depression stage it is perfectly healthy to do so when grieving. After all the energy expelled and the mental anguish of the other stages, depression gives you time to reflect and recover. Taking ample time to feel the loneliness and isolation make it easier to re-enter the world when you are ready.

When going through depression, avoid people who encourage you to "snap out of it." For one, you cannot control your emotions that way. Instead, let yourself feel the despair and emptiness– just as you let yourself feel the other stages. This is a significant period of reflection and recuperation.

7. ACCEPTANCE

As a person adjusts to life without the person they grieve, the depression and other extreme feelings fade away. Common signs of acceptance include:

- Restructuring life without the person

- Cleaning out the loved one's personal items.

- Working on financial and social problems

- Seeking out old relationships and support systems

- Beginning new projects or hobbies

Acceptance does not equate to happiness. Rather, acceptance is the stage where a grieving person makes a conscious decision to move on and work towards a feeling of normality again. After a significant loss, a person rarely feels the same way they were before again. Acceptance occurs when a person stops looking toward the past and focuses on the future.

Chapter 17
Reacting to the Grief or Loss

People often respond to their grief in several different ways. No two people will experience a loss in the same manner. many of the clients I counsel share with me how their initial reaction to their loss is to simply shut down. I let them know it's okay to take a break but even though the process of overcoming their grief and loss can be difficult they must be willing to go through it to get through it.

Some of the reactions I have seen my clients experience or:

(1) Displacement of their feelings

(2) Bottling up of the grief

(3) Projections of anger toward doctors, nurses, hospitals, caregivers, and family members.

    (4) Projection of guilt as above, feeling the need to punish oneself, or others ('I deserve this').

    (5) Helplessness— difficulty in coping with new situations that may require behavior change.

(6), feelings of shame and embarrassment, especially common where death is by suicide.

Chapter 18

The Accepting of God's Will

(More Excerpts from "THE EMPTY QUIVER")

Accepting God's will for our life is often a very difficult task for anyone, especially when it goes against what we want or desire for ourselves and for those whom we love and care for.

Overcoming any challenge is difficult. Overcoming drug addictions, alcoholism, depression, the loss of a child, and any other kind of loss often requires a long and hard-fought process. This is a day-by-day process. We do not always know why God takes us on the paths He does, but we know that just like He took the children of Israel from the wilderness to the Promised Land, it is sometimes a slow and tedious journey. Overcoming pain and hurt are never easy to do without the help of God. And even with God, it takes prayer and much faith to overcome.

Chapter 19
Moving Forward

After experiencing a major loss our initial reaction is, I can't take it. I will never get over this. The challenge is to be able to move beyond the feeling that I will never get over my loss and how I can move forward.

Many of my clients who were experiencing grief also found themselves dealing with depression. There are different levels of grief as well as different levels of depression a person can, and often will, experience as they process the loss they experience.

For many Christians, it is unthinkable for them to see a therapist, but as a Christian, as well as a secular therapist, I have had many Christians, reluctantly come to me as a last resort when everything else they have tried has failed.

Learning to accept the loss is one of the first steps in moving forward. Do not be afraid or ashamed to admit you are hurting. Be willing to reach out to friends, family members, the clergy, or a therapist for help.

For anyone to move forward from their grief, anxiety, depression, or even trauma there must be a conscious desire and effort to do so.

STAGES OF CHANGE

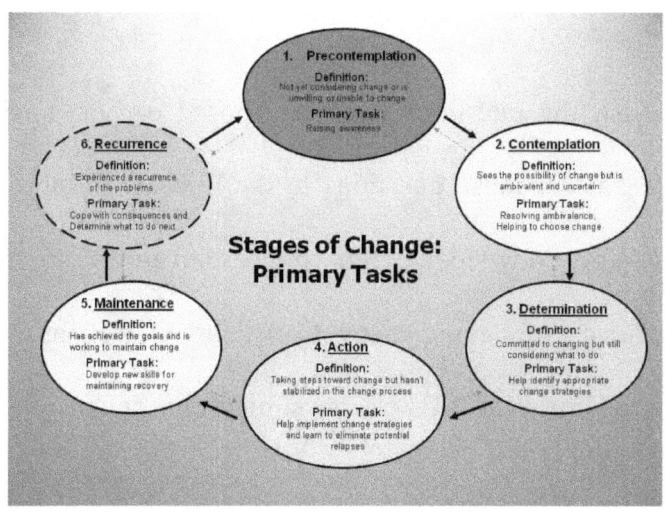

Chapter 20
Grief and Loss in the Church

Now we come to the part where we previously discussed myths in the church and questions, I am often asked regarding Christians dealing with depression, anxiety, grief, and trauma. Many Christians are more apt to have a harder time adjusting to grief and loss than non-Christians. There are several reasons for this.

Let us revisit the questions that were posed earlier. I will attempt to answer these questions to the best of my ability according to my knowledge of the word of God along with my vast experience of having many Christians as well as not Christians ask me many of the same similar questions.

Chapter 21
Questions I Am Often Asked About Grief Loss and Depression

- Can Christians Become Depressed?
- If I suffer from Depression and am I Saved?
- Are Prayers Alone Able to Deliver Me from Depression?
- If I'm Struggling with Depression can Fast Along Help?
- Should a child of God constantly be worrying?
- What does it mean if a child of God is Overly Fearful?
- Once I am diagnosed as being Depressed does that mean I will always have it?
- How long will I struggle with it?
- If I see a therapist about my Grief or Depression does that mean I do not have faith?
- Can I continue to Minister if I am depressed?

Can Christians Become Depressed?

Christians are not immune to the everyday challenges of life and can easily become overloaded with the cares of this life and not focus on God.

The answer is yes Christians can and many have gone through some form or another of depression even if it only lasted a short period.

Some of the reasons Christians as well as non Christians experience depressions are:

- Experiencing a sudden loss
- Overburdening themselves (Slow down)
- Lack of emotional support
- Lack of finances
- Change in their Health.

- Experiencing a sense of helplessness when addressing their own needs or that of others they deeply care for

- Associating with negative speaking people
- Having feelings of being inadequate
- Being missed understood
- Not being able to communicate with others correctly
- Having poor conflict-resolution skills

If I suffer from Depression and am I Saved?

As stated earlier you can experience depression and still be saved. Depression can often be managed with prayer, therapy, and in some cases the right medication.
There are many instances in the bible where men have shown a proclivity to experience some level of depression.

"Oh that my head were waters, and mine eyes a fountain of tears, that I might weep day and night for the slain of the daughter of my people!"   Jeremiah 9:1 KJV

Are Prayers Alone Able to Deliver Me from Depression?

As a minister of the gospel, I can say unequivocally that a person can be delivered from many cases of depression through prayer. However, as a therapist, there are cases where there is a need for prayer coupled with therapy or medication that would be the best course of action.

If I'm Struggling with Depression can A Fast Along Help Me?

There are times when challenges in life are not a one-stop cure.

Sometimes Jesus would touch them and they were healed and there were times they were asked to go and see the priest.

Should a child of God constantly be worrying?

Worrying is defined as:

": mental distress or agitation resulting from concern usually for something impending or anticipated: anxiety. an instance or occurrence of such distress or agitation. a cause of worry: trouble, difficulty."

There are times when we all may find ourselves worrying over something but this should be short-lived. There are several scriptures we can turn to that encourages of not to worry or be anxious about anything.

"Casting all your care upon him; for he careth for you."
1 Peter 5:7 KJV

"Be anxious for nothing, but in everything by prayer and supplication, with thanksgiving, let your requests be made known to God"
Phillipians 4:6 NKJV

Proverbs 3:5-6 KJV

What does it mean for a child of God to be Overly Fearful?

Fear has been defined as faith in reverse. We should continue to put our trust in God and not be fearful of anything. An over amount of fear is what causes stress and then high blood pressure for a lot of people. The Bible tells us:

"There is no fear in love; but perfect love casteth out fear: because fear hath torment. He that feareth is not made perfect in love"

1 John 4:18 JKV

"For God hath not given us the spirit of fear; but of power, and of love, and of a sound mind"
2 Timothy 1:7

Once I am diagnosed as being Depressed does that mean I will always have it?

The answer to that in most cases in 'NO". Many factors may cause a person to experience mild to severe depression.

How long will I struggle with it?

This is a more difficult question because no one can completely know the will of God. The scriptures tell us:

For this thing, I besought the Lord thrice, that it might depart from me.

And he said unto me, My grace is sufficient for thee: for my strength is made perfect in weakness. Most gladly therefore will I rather glory in my infirmities, that the power of Christ may rest upon me."

2 Corinthians 12:7-9 KJV

We must do as the scripture admonishes us, to" pray without ceasing."

We cannot put a time limit on anything we go through but be confident to know the grace of God is sufficient to take us through it.

If I see a therapist about my Grief or Depression does that mean I do not have faith?

Being a therapist myself, believe me, it does not mean a person does not have faith whenever he or she seeks out wisdom from someone with knowledge and expertise that you may not have.

The scriptures tell us:

"Even so faith, if it hath not works, is dead, being alone."

James 2:17 KJV

We must realize when we need help in an area of our lives and never be ashamed to go and get the proper help we need from the proper sources.

Can I continue to Minister if I am depressed?

I would like to share my personal story of where I experienced stress and kept ministering. I felt as though I had to show my church that even when you are hurting you still have to come to church.

My mom was sick and dying of cancer. She was in one city and I was in another about three hours away. Even though I was hurting and experiencing tremendous sadness I kept on ministering to everyone and just kept my hurt and pain to myself. I did this because I thought that was what was expected of a good pastor. What I was doing was good for the church membership but it was forcing me to take on more than what I should have been doing.

This is a good place to talk about one of the most important parts of good health is our self-care. While I was helping everyone out, I was burning myself out and having negative thoughts due to not getting enough rest. It might sound strange to say, that even though I was feeling feelings of depression I still maintained my position in ministry. I was hurting myself. I would have to say if I had an opportunity to do it all over again, I would have spent a little more time on myself and focused more on what was going on with my mom.

An important part of an effective ministry is having a good support system and allowing them to function on their own in your absence. Having a good support system will help to ease the load and in turn, can minimize the anxiety or depression you may be experiencing.

Chapter 22
You Do Not Have To Be Superman - Allowing You To Be You

An individual's ability to perform his or her duties must be decided truthfully by the person who is experiencing depression.

After the eventual death of my mom, no one knew, or at least I felt that no one knew the amount of pain and depression I was going through. At the time all I wanted to do was to be alone and hold in my feelings. As I was hurting, I realize I was going through some of the same experiences that I had gone through at the death of my son. There were things I went through and things that were said to me that triggered what I went through with my son.

Knowing my mother was at death's door and that there was very little I could do, was very, very difficult for me. I found myself having a hard time staying focused at times and at other times shedding tears at the thought of her not being around.

We somehow have this ideal that Christians, especially ministers, must be Superman or Superwoman. We do not have to be either we just must learn to work in the capacity for which God has given us. I think too many people take on more than what they should, do and this can easily be a contributing cause to their depression.

I remember going to church and ministering right after the passing of my mom as though nothing had happened. (I felt that this was what was expected of me). I now realized because of what I was going through it would have been acceptable to have taken a break if at least only for a week or so.)

I remember the struggle I went through internally as I tried to minister when everything within me was hurting. Again, I felt that this was what a minister, pastor, or leader should do, "Just be strong". When you are suffering any mental pain or hurt being strong does not mean checking all the right boxes at the right time. Being strong means knowing yourself and operating within your limitations with the help of God.

It is important to know there are many types of depression as mentioned earlier. A lot depends on the level of depression, grief, and anxiety you are experiencing.

In my case, I continue to minister, and I felt at the time I was doing a good job, but the truth of the matter is as I heard someone say, "A man or woman ought to know their limitations. It is important to know when enough is enough. We have had a lot of good leaders with good intentions that are in the grave today or are so stressed out because they were or are currently putting too much on themselves. they were not able to perform at their optimum peak and were only stressing themselves out.

Chapter 23
Addressing Trauma and PTSD

According to HelpGuide. Org, *"Emotional and psychological trauma is the result of extraordinarily stressful events that shatter your sense of security, making you feel helpless in a dangerous world. Psychological trauma can leave you struggling with upsetting emotions, memories, and anxiety that won't go away. It can also leave you feeling numb, disconnected, and unable to trust other people.*

Coping with the trauma of a natural or manmade disaster can present unique challenges—even if you weren't directly involved in the event. In fact, while it's highly unlikely any of us will ever be the direct victims of a terrorist attack, plane crash, or mass shooting, for example, we're all regularly bombarded by horrific images on social media and news sources of those people who have been. Viewing these images over and over can overwhelm your nervous system and create <u>traumatic stress</u>."

For many of my clients who have experienced trauma, helping them to overcome the pain and hurt of trauma is not an easy process. The challenge is there may be several things that you and I would consider normal that can trigger the trauma they once experienced. An example would be a client who shared with me how whenever the July 4th Holiday comes around, he often finds himself bald up into the fetal position at the sounds of the fireworks which reminds him of being on the battlefield in the military.

When a person is experiencing PSTD it is as if they are reliving the hurt and the pain they experience all over again in real time.

Pastors And Depression

*A recent survey from Lifeway Research found nearly **1 in 5 (18%)** pastors deal with depression to some degree. If there are five churches in your town or on your street, one pastor is dealing with depression. If you attend a church with five or more pastors, statistically, one of them is dealing with depression.*

LifeWay Research
Dealing with Depression When You're the Pastor

Insights| Personal Development | Aug 22, 2022
Damir Samatkulov photo | Unsplash

Many pastors struggle with depression to some degree.

By Marty Duren

Lifeway Research surveys indicate **pastoral struggles with personal mental illness (including depression) are on the**

rise. Pastors who affirmed having a diagnosed "mental illness of any kind" rose from 12% in 2014 to 17% in 2021.

Testing Your Knowledge

1. <u>Is grief a normal reaction?</u>
2. <u>Mourning and grief are the same. True or False?</u>
3. <u>Anger is an unusual response to grief. True or False?</u>
4. <u>Who has more difficulty dealing with major loss?</u>
5. <u>What is bereavement?</u>
6. <u>What is anticipatory grief?</u>
7. <u>Should a grieving person minimize feelings?</u>
8. <u>Crying can help resolve grief. True or False?</u>

Tips For Supporting Someone Who is Experiencing a Loss:

1. Validate their feelings
2. Be Non- Judgmental
3. Let them take the lead-take your cues from their reactions
4. Be Present – You don't have to feel like you have to always say something
5. Be willing to just Listen-Hear them out.
6. Be a comforting shoulder to lean on
7. Let them know you are available for them
8. Be Patient
9. Be Empathetic
10. Let them know you are holding them up in prayer continually

Chapter 24
Tips for working through your Grief, Anxiety, Depression, and Trauma

Journaling-
- I encourage my client to keep a journal of their feelings. This can be very helpful in processing their negative thought patterns.

- **Positive Self-Talk-**

We can sometimes be our worse enemy through the negative self-talk we tell ourselves daily. Do not allow yourself to constantly be putting yourself down or listening to others who are putting you down but are not trying to help you.

- **Live in the moment-**
- **Do not rob the joy of today for worrying about tomorrow**
- **Mindfulness Thinking**

A mental state that is achieved by focusing one's awareness on the present moment, while calmly acknowledging and accepting one's feelings, thoughts, and bodily sensations, is used as a therapeutic technique.

- Prayer and Meditation

- Allow yourself some quiet time
- Allow yourself some alone time
- Do not be afraid to talk with a Pastor, counselor, therapist, or even a close friend

- Self-Care

- Exercise

Chapter 25
Suicide Ideations

The thought process of having ideas, or ruminations about the possibility of ending one's own life. It is not a diagnosis but is a symptom of some mental disorders and can also occur in response to adverse events without the presence of a mental disorder.

On suicide risk scales, the range of suicidal ideation varies from fleeting thoughts to detailed planning. Passive suicidal ideation is thinking about not wanting to live or imagining being dead. Active suicidal ideation involves preparation to commit suicide or forming a plan to do so.

If you feel someone you know is considering suicide do not be afraid to ask them directly "Have you had thoughts of taking your life?" It is always better to err on the safe side rather than have regrets later. Studies have shown that asking these questions will not make that person more apt to commit suicide. If anything, it shows them that someone is concerned about them,

Another important thing when speaking with someone who may be considering suicide is to ask them if they know how they would commit suicide. If they have a plan, they are more likely to follow up on their plan to commit suicide.

Chapter 26

My Crisis Plan

*This is an actual plan that you would use in a time of crisis. You may want to fill this in before you find yourself dealing with any kind of crisis.

When I am sad, I can do this:

_____
_____
_____
_____

When I need someone to talk with, I can Call:

_____   ___ ___-___

_____   ___ ___-___

_____   ___ ___-___

What are some positive things I can think about that will put a smile on my face?

List some of the things you are most thankful for.

Chapter 27

Resources for Getting Mental Health Help

Mental Health Charities Making a Big Impact [Updated 2022]
- 1. National Alliance on Mental Illness (NAMI)
- 2. Mental Health Innovations (MHI)
- 3. Mental Health America (MHA)
- 4. Rethink Mental Health Incorporated
- 5. National Institute for Mental Health (NIMH)
- 6. Child Mind Institute
- 7. American Foundation for Suicide Prevention
- 8. Strong Minds

Hope for Sadness (churchescare.com)

988 Suicide and Crisis Lifeline | Federal Communications Commission (fcc.gov)

National Hotline for Mental Health Crises and Suicide Prevention | NAMI: National Alliance on Mental Illness

Home | NAMI: National Alliance on Mental Illness

- **Organizations for General Mental Health**
- **American Psychiatric Association (APA)**
- **American Psychological Association (APA)**
- **Bring Change to Mind (BC2M)**
- **HelpGuide**
- **MentalHealth.gov**

- **Mental Health America (MHA)**
- **National Alliance on Mental Illness (NAMI)**
- **National Institute of Mental Health (NIMH)**
- **Substance Abuse & Mental Health Services Administration (SAMHSA)**
- **Disorder-Specific Mental Health Charities**
- **Anxiety & Depression Association of America (ADAA)**
- **National Eating Disorders Association (NEDA)**
- **National Institute of Alcoholism & Alcohol Abuse (NIAAA)**
- **988 Suicide & Crisis Lifeline | SAMHSA**

*If you are experiencing difficult thoughts call: 988

*Emergency Number 911

NOTES:

References

Grief Loss Recovery – Hope and Health Through Creative Grieving [Grief Loss Recovery – Hope and Health Through Creative Grieving]. (n.d.). https://www.recover-from-grief.com/

Stoecklein, K. (2020). *Fear gone wild: A story of mental illness, suicide, and hope through loss.* Nelson Books.

Trenton, N. (2021). *Stop overthinking: 23 techniques to relieve stress, stop negative spirals, declutter your mind, and focus on the present.* Nick Trenton.

Walton, A. (2018). *The Window to Understanding And Building Healthy Relationships.* Walton Publishing.

Walton, A., PH.D. (2017). *The Empty Quiver.* Walton Publishing.

www.ingramcontent.com/pod-product-compliance
Lightning Source LLC
Chambersburg PA
CBHW061944220426
43662CB00012B/2023